Light relief between grades

Spaß und Entspannung mit leichten Originalstücken für Altsaxophon *Zweiter Schwierigkeitsgrad*

Plaisir et détente avec des pièces originales simples pour saxophone alto *Niveau 2*

Alto saxophone part

Pam Wedgwood

GW00493885

FABER _ff_ MUSIC

Foreword

Up-Grade! is a collection of new pieces and duets in a wide variety of styles for alto saxophonists of any age. This book is designed to be especially useful to students who have passed Grade 2 and would like a break before plunging into the syllabus for Grade 3.

Whether you're looking for stimulating material to help bridge the gap between grades, or simply need a bit of light relief, I hope you'll enjoy **Up-Grade!**

Pam Wedgwood

Contents

© 2000 by Faber Music Ltd
First published in 2000 by Faber Music Ltd
Bloomsbury House 74–77 Great Russell Street London WC1B 3DA
Cover illustration by Stik
Music processed by Jackie Leigh
Printed in England by Caligraving Ltd
All rights reserved

ISBN10: 0-571-52072-3
EAN13: 978-0-571-52072-5

To buy Faber Music publications or to find out about the full range of titles available
please contact your local music retailer or Faber Music sales enquiries:

Faber Music Limited, Burnt Mill, Elizabeth Way, Harlow, CM20 2HX England
Tel: +44 (0)1279 82 89 82   Fax: +44 (0)1279 82 89 83
Email: sales@fabermusic.com   fabermusic.com

1. Eclipse

Pamela Wedgwood

2. Scale-learning Blues!

Pamela Wedgwood

3. Symphony no. 40 in G minor (1st movement)

W.A. Mozart

© 2000 by Faber Music Ltd.

4. Rosie

Pamela Wedgwood

5. The Easy Winners

Scott Joplin

6. Just for You

With reflection – at a steady tempo ♩ = 66

Pamela Wedgwood

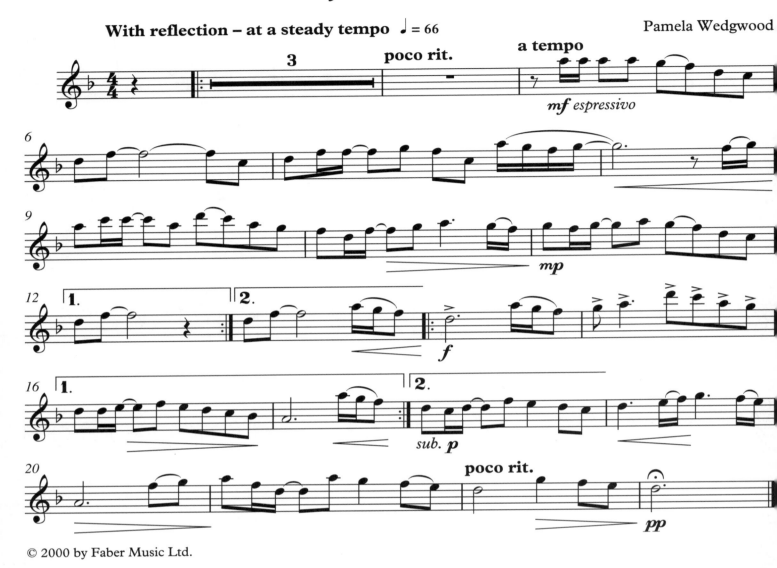

7. The Mango Walk

Jamaican folksong

Lively ♩ = 120

8. Plaza de Toros

Pamela Wedgwood

9. Journey to Saturn

Pamela Wedgwood

10. Siberian Galop

Pamela Wedgwood

11. Five Jive

Pamela Wedgwood

12. All in a day's work!

As brisk as possible ♩ = 120–148

Pamela Wedgwood

13. Free and Easy

14. Flibbertigibbet

Pamela Wedgwood